A Simple Guide for Writing and Publishing

by

James Kelly

A Simple Guide for Writing and Publishing

Constructed and Written
by
James Kelly

With contributions by Cynthia L. De Boer

10 Digit ISBN 1-886726-11-6
13 Digit ISBN 978-1-886726-11-6

Copyright ©2018

Mammoth Star Publishing
5125 W. Oquendo Road
Suite#12
Las Vegas, Nevada 89118

www.aspectsofwriting.com

All Rights Reserved
No part of this book may be reproduced, scanned or distributed in printed or electronic format without the expressed written permission from the publisher.

Table of Contents

PURPOSE AND PASSION .... Page 1
SOCIAL MEDIA .... Page 5
WRITING STYLES AND LAYOUT ……...… Page 7
FORMATTING ………………………….... Page 10
EDITING ……………………………..… Page 17
TRADITIONAL PUBLISHERS VERSUS
SELF-PUBLISHING ……………………….. Page 22
THE AUTHORS WEBSITE …………………. Page 29
FUNDING YOUR PROJECT …………….. Page 32
BECOMING THE AUTHOR
– BOOK SIGNINGS ……………………….. Page 38
CHECK LIST FOR PUBLISHING …………. Page 40
IN CONCLUSION …………………….…... Page 45
ADDITIONAL WEBSITES
WORTH YOUR WHILE ………………..…… Page 46

A Simple Guide for Writing and Publishing

PURPOSE AND PASSION

Finding your passion may be easier than you think. I know one author who was a retired FBI agent who had been writing for years. First, as an article writer for science magazines as he was getting his degree in forensic science, then as an agent writing his reports for the various cases to which he had been assigned. Another author, Joyce K. Gatschenberger, was an RN for over thirty years. Again, writing reports was a part of her career. Both found a way of turning that passion for writing into becoming an author. In other words, the passion was always there, they just redirected it. Cynthia L. De Boer wrote her book, *Me, Myself and Eye*, based on her own experience with disabilities.

I began writing as a hobby when I was in my early twenties and unemployed. Journalism was not my class studies, nor did I obtain a college degree. Nonetheless, I had a knack for storytelling. I had always considered myself a creator. However, the reality is, once you put your idea on paper, you are now a writer.

Joanne Penn of www.thecreativepenn.com offers a great insight of what is meant by Purpose and Passion in writing.

Putting an idea on paper is not always as simple as it sounds. I used to tell my guests who attended my "Aspects of Writing" series back in 1996 to "Write the first sentence." If you can get something on paper – anything – you have a direction from which to proceed. It does not matter if you move forward or backward with the idea. The most important thing is that you start.

Identify Your Passion

One definition of passion according to the Merriam Webster Dictionary is - an object of desire or deep interest.

Know your strengths and write to them. Often, our strengths and passions intersect, but not always.

In the context of writing, passion might mean many things. It can mean a sense of purpose - my writing will make a difference and change the world. Alternatively, it can be love of the subject you are writing about. You may feel excitement about your project that if you don't write you'll explode. Letting your project get you all fired up is a good thing!

Identify Your Purpose

The definition of purpose according to the Meriam Webster Dictionary is - something set up as an object or end to be attained.

What is it that you hope to accomplish? Can your book be described in one or two sentences? Figure out why you are writing. Is it to make money, change the world, to make someone laugh, or to just entertain family and friends? What do you want your reader to take away from your project once they have closed the back cover?

Some writers do it for accolades, others to influence the way we think. The list is seemingly endless whether it is to teach, inspire, motivate, criticize, make change, to report, make money, or to tell a story. The important thing is to discover your own reasons, so you can use them.

Putting Them Together

When you put purpose with passion, the magic really happens. You will find that writing becomes more enjoyable. There is little doubt, the more you write, the more you will learn. Your writing skills will improve, and you will be more enthusiastic about what you write.

Finding the Right Software

Now that you have discovered your purpose and passion, think about what software you may use to write your book. Several are available to make the writing process easier. Here are just a few: Microsoft Word, Scrivener, Google Docs, FocusWriter, yWriter, Evernote, Hemingway Editor, and Pages or Ulysses for Mac users. Most all are free.

Take the time to check out each if you are not already using one. Discover what your weaknesses and strengths are, and then make your determination. My advice is to stick with the book writing software that gives you the best results in terms of saving you money, time, and frustration. If you are a scriptwriter for movies or television, you might try Final Draft, Screenwriter, or my favorite, Fade In.

Keep writing–keep it simple–but most of all, enjoy the creative process.

SOCIAL MEDIA

Setting up your social media accounts may be one of the first things you will want to do before even starting your manuscript. It can take a while to build your friends or following on each account, and there are multiple platforms out there, i.e. Facebook, Pinterest, Instagram, Tumblr, YouTube, Blogger, Goodreads and more. You may also want to include an e-mail-based campaign for your work. Having a Goodreads account is important. This is where readers often go to learn about your book and read reviews.

How important is it to understand and use social media? Very important! If you are a first-time author, comprehending the various social media platforms is essential. Building your network of fans and friends via the internet is one of the quickest and easiest ways.

Navigating the different social media outlets may seem daunting, but it is necessary to take the plunge. Posting photos and announcements of your events is essential. Once you have established a base of friends on your social media platforms, you will find this is also a great way of networking or connecting with the author community. They will share their ideas, and you can share ideas with them.

See where they have or are holding book signings. Look at their events calendar and take notice of where they have conducted radio and television interviews.

Here are a few reasons why it is important to start your "friends" list before publishing.

Australian author, Pat Ritter, posts a page a day to his fan base. Every time he starts a new novel, he shares a page each morning with his 10,000 plus e-mail readers who are eager to see what he has written next. This is a great way to get feedback useful for editing and developing the characters and story.

Many authors I know offer free eBooks for a set period after a book's release. EBook sales can generate bound book sales if the reader likes what they read. Freebies always attract attention.

Once your book is ready, consider a live campaign to let people know your book is in the process of being released. People want to know what you have been working on for the past few months. This is a great way to invite them to your event or to listen to your radio interview.

WRITING STYLES AND LAYOUT

Writer's Digest offers a few suggestions regarding writing styles and layouts.

Every piece of writing has its own structure. Start with the skeleton and then build from there. It is important to have a uniform foundation upon which you, the writer, and the creator, can build something unique.

Here are six common writing structures.

1. Evaluative is a structure that introduces a problem, and then the pros and cons are weighed - for example, when writing a text or e-mail to a friend for advice.

2. Categorical, according to the Webster Dictionary, means - involving, according with, or considered with respect to specific categories. Categorical writing can be used to debate, convince, or argue and important topic, such as a political speech, or the cover letter for a job application.

3. Comparative structure is like evaluative. Comparative structure is used when there are more layers to the situation. For instance, if you were to write a speech for a debate team

you would want to explain the various reasons why you feel your point is stronger than that of your opponent's. Another example would be to use comparative structure to explain in a letter to your congressional representative why you disagree with current legislation introduced in Washington.

4. Causal structure, or casual augment, is when the writer focuses on how something has caused or has possibly led to a problem. This type of structure may seem like Comparative structure. However, it differs in that it does not involve weighing options against one another. Causal structure discusses the causes and effects regarding a topic or issue in that order. For example, how something has come about, such as the contributing factors to global warming. Causal structure can also be used to explain why you are terminating a contract.

5. Most authors write chronologically. Chronological structure is when the focus is on telling the story, rather than the result; a sequence of events that will lead up to the ending. Most short stories and novels are written in chronological fashion.

6. Sequential structure is like Chronological. It is normally used to structure how-to and the systematic process. When writing sequentially,

you might use words like, "First," "Next," "Then," and "Finally" to clarify your instructions.

FORMATTING

Formatting may not be the daunting task imagined. At least it does not have to be.

For Grammar and Writing Style, I suggest using the EIA Writing Style Guide (free online and included in your folder), the Gregg Reference Manual, or the Chicago Manual of Style. They are a great way of understanding the standard explanation of the following:

1. Abbreviations: Example, you may allow continued to be abbreviated in a title name. If so, you might want it to be capitalized and put in parenthesis, like this: (Cont.), or lower case and no parentheses, etc.

2. Acronyms: Which ones are acceptable and when? An acronym is a word formed from the initial letter or letters of a group of words such as FBI (Federal Bureau of Investigation).

3. Bulleted Points: Bullet points are visually attractive and make it easy for a reader to locate important information. There are a few things you may want to ask yourself before using them. Should the list start with a capital letter? Should the bullets contain punctuation

marks? If yes, how, and when should they be punctuated?

4. Capitalization: Should a word four letters or more in a title (such as with or that) be capitalized? This can be tricky. When it comes to a title, for instance, most words that are four letters or more probably should be capitalized.

5. Punctuation: Understanding when and where to punctuate can be problematic. For example, whether or not to use a comma before the word "and" in lists such as x, y, and z, or whether to put a space before and after a dash in a sentence–such as the dash that precedes this statement. Knowing when to use quotation marks with continued narrative is important. You may even want to identify when to use an em dash (–, which is the width of an m) verses an en dash (-, which is the width of an n).

6. Voice or tone: Essentially, your voice is like putting your personality on paper. You will need to know when to use a passive or active voice. Be careful of using a snarky or condescending tone that may seem otherwise unappealing.

7. Writing style: This refers to the way a writer presents his or her thoughts on paper. Word choice descriptions define the way you write.

Expository writing is objective, or free from personal opinion. Descriptive writing is when an author is trying to paint a mental picture. Persuasive writing is when the author is trying to convince the reader to see his or her point-of-view. Creative writing is technically considered any writing of original composition.

Formatting Style Guide Examples:

1. Font: Fonts can be important. They can attract your reader, and even influence the meaning of a sentence or word. This is particularly true for titles of a book. Other examples of using the right or proper font are what style to use for a transcript, onscreen text, menu items, or a various type of book (i.e. science fiction, romance or a children's book).

2. Graphics: They can be important, depending on the type of book. Obviously, graphics are important when writing a children's picture book, the cover layout, or enhancing a story with pictorials.

3. Line Spacing: The amount of line spacing required in, before, or after a paragraph. This can vary depending on taste and, again, type of book. I suggest you look at traditionally

published manuscripts to get an idea of the current trend.

4. Page Layout: What page layout should be used? The objective of a design layout is to communicate information clearly and effectively to your reader. Most publishing websites offer free page layouts, which can be downloaded, based on book size and type of book.

5. Space after a Period: How do you determine if one or two spaces should be used after a period? In the past, two spaces were used when the main means for writing a manuscript was a typewriter. Only one font was available, and all the letters were monospaced, or took the same amount of space. With the invention of the computer, word processing programs began offering various fonts. Each font was programmed to space characters proportionally. Most computer fonts will automatically give enough room between sentences with one space. Therefore, according to nearly all stylebooks, including The Associated Press Stylebook and the Chicago Manual of Style, always use a single space after a period.

6. Styles: This can be preset in most programs that are used to write a manuscript. It is easier

to determine what style names and characteristics are going to be used before beginning your book.

You could hire a professional, but you really do not need to. Once you have your manuscript written in a program like Microsoft Word, there are tools within Word that will make your life easier and more efficient. Most of the writing programs today offer the same tools found in high-end layout programs. When you download a template from a printer or POD publisher, often they will have preset styles in the format.

Perhaps you may wish to download a template and work from there. I, on the other hand, usually write my text, then copy and paste my work into the already formatted template. Just highlight the text, right click, then paste your work using the "A" in word, or "Keep text only" into the already formatted page.

A style in Word is simply a way to capture all the formatting for a particular piece of text so it can be named, edited, and used for all other pieces of text that are similar.

If you are like me, you may sometimes find it difficult to understand how the various programs work, regardless of how easy they are supposed to be. I suggest visiting YouTube.com and click on a step-by-step video about formatting. There is a video for everything these days.

When it comes to formatting, consider these platforms, **Kindle Direct Publishing**, **Barnes and Noble**, and **Ingram Spark**. They offer the various templates I mentioned earlier that can be downloaded and used. You will want to publish with Ingram Spark to get your book into the bigger markets like Barnes and Noble. When you place your book with Ingram, make sure to choose 55% markup and returnable in order for the major bookstores to order and carry your book. You will make less royalty, but you will gain more visibility. You can still place your book with Amazon; just do not chose "expanded distribution" with **Kindle Direct Publishing**.

For the eBook format, I highly recommend **Draft2Digital**.Not only do they create your book for free, they only charge a ten percent (10%) commission on your book once it sells online. You get 90% royalty on all books sold. In addition, they use your Word file to format your book for all the eBook outlets. There is no need to create a separate Pdf file. **Draft2Digital** will also post your book to all the various outlets like Barnes and Noble, Amazon, Kobo, iBooks, Scribd, Playster, OverDrive, Tolino,

24Symbols and more. **Kindle Direct** offers their own format to publish on Amazon. If you place your eBook version solely with **Draft2Digital**, they will distribute your eBook to all the major outlets like Barnes and Nobel and Amazon.

To learn more about **Draft2Digital**, and how it works: https://www.draft2digital.com

EDITING

Types of Editing

There are several types of editing. You may or may not need them all. The terms can be confusing to a new author, especially because the terms are often used interchangeably and may have different meanings within the industry. I suggest, that when hiring an editor, always speak to him or her about exactly what the editing includes. Always check with your editor and put in writing what his or her services cover, regardless of the terms used.

1. Copyediting is also a form of line editing. It is a light form of editing that applies to a professional polished book. The editor will review your work; fix any mechanical errors in spelling, grammar, and punctuation. Copyediting is often the least-expensive version of editing. There are some professionals who will divide copyediting and line editing into two separate edits. Copyediting is lighter; grammar-only edit. Line Editing is a more intense look at the meaning of each sentence. Always clarify with your editor what is included in his or her copyedit.

2. Line editing is often used interchangeably with copyediting. However, in line editing, the

editor looks at your book line by line and analyzes each sentence. The editor considers word choice, the power and meaning of a sentence, the syntax and whether a sentence needs to be trimmed or tightened.

3. Mechanical editing refers to the application of a style, such as The Chicago Manual of Style or Associated Press (AP) Style. The editor looks at the punctuation, capitalization, spelling, abbreviations, and any other style rules. An editor will often include copyediting.

4. Substantive editing involves the organization and presentation of a work. The editor will clarify and tighten each chapter, scene, paragraph, and sentence level. Substantive editing is sometimes referred to as line editing and can be confused with developmental editing.

5. Development editing is when the editor looks deeply at the organization and strength of a book; in other words, "The Big Picture." The editor will consider everything from pacing to characters, point of view, tense, plot, subplots, and dialogue. This is when the weak links are exposed and questioned. The editor will scrutinize the order, flow, and consistency of the work. This may include questions about the right number of chapters, are the chapters and

paragraphs in the right order, are there any places in the book where the pacing lags, is there a hole in the information or story presented, and are the characters likable? This type of editing considers all the aspects of a manuscript that make the book readable and enjoyable. This form of editing can be more time intensive and costly. Nonetheless, it is worth the investment if you are serious about succeeding as an author.

Types of Editors

There are several types of Editors. However, most are those assigned to the bigger publishing houses. If you are self-publishing, you will probably only deal with one editor who does it all, and/or maybe a proofreader. I always recommend a separate proofer, even if the editor agrees to do it all.

1. What is an Acquisitions Editor? An acquisition editor is responsible for bringing new titles to their publishing house. Acquisitions editors weed through proposals and manuscripts that land on their desks. Acquisitions editors also actively search for writers to complete certain projects.

2. A Project Editor oversees all facets of book production. They often deal with the writer to make sure the project is proceeding on

schedule. The copy editor, developmental editor and proofreader often work under the project editor to keep the book moving through production in a timely fashion.

3. A Developmental Editor works with the author to produce a publishable book. The Developmental Editor will identify problems with the plot in fiction books, and guide authors through the process of taking raw material and turning it into readable and compelling text in non-fiction titles.

4. The Copy Editor is also called the line editor. He or she will go through manuscript to correct the grammar and sentence structure and improve the flow of ideas. Their purpose is to resolve any inconsistencies. Copy editors must have an exceptional eye for errors and the patience to wade through manuscripts line by line. Their job is also to determine if the manuscript fits together in a logical way.

5. The Proofreader is a vital part of the editing process, especially for the self-published author. Most people imagine that editors do all the proofreading required of our text, and you may have a contract for your editor to do just that. Proofreading is essential. The Proofreader will catch errors that all other eyes have

missed. The Proofreader is the one who wraps the editing process up.

TRADITIONAL PUBLISHERS VERSUS SELF-PUBLISHING

The difference between self-publishing and traditional publishing.

Most of the time, a traditional publisher will handle the marketing, distribution, and warehousing of your book. There is generally little or no expense to the author. This is because the mainstream publisher makes a greater profit from the sale of your book. After all, they are taking the bigger risk. The average royalty is between 8 to 15% paid to the author for each book sold.

Whereas with self-publishing, depending on which publisher or platform you choose, much of the work and expenses falls on your shoulders. The biggest differences as a self-published author are, you control when the book is published, and you retain all the rights to your book, and therefore receive 100 % of the profits.

Which one is right for you?

This will depend on your personal goal. If it is just a hobby, perhaps a vanity press might be your best option. If you are writing memoir, book of poetry, or family history, you are limiting your audience. Therefore, a POD (Print on Demand) publishing house might be your best choice. Most are nonreturnable and you do not have to store any unsold books. Simply order the amount you need when you need them.

If you have a visible platform, or an established audience, POD has several options, whether you decide to offer a printed version, eBook version or an audio.

You need to consider if getting your book to press is time-sensitive, keep in mind a commercial publishing company can take up to 18 months to get your book from manuscript and into production.

Consider this as well, if don't have an online presence, don't have the time to spend presenting your book on the internet, dislike social media, or simply don't know how to find or reach your readers, the traditional publisher might be the best route. This is especially true if you want to be in a brick-and-mortar type bookstore and prefer to someone else handle the marketing for you.

Simply weigh your options, and then decide.

Self-Publishing — for some that may be the best choice.

The Pro's

After numerous attempts to land an agent, manager or traditional publisher, many authors try their hand at self-publishing. Others have reverted to self-publishing after their mid-stream publisher has gone out of business. A few more have simple chosen to branch out on their own after their traditional publisher refused to let then write and publish in a different genre.

It is important to note that independently published eBooks on Amazon Kindle account for more than double the representation of the top five Traditional Publishers.

According to authorearnings.com, the top five traditional publishers now account for less than a quarter of all eBook sales on Amazon. Between February 2014 and January 2016, it is estimated that the big five traditional publishers are making less than a quarter of the dollars earned by creatives for their eBook sales. Let's break it down this way; four of Amazon's overall Top 10 Best Selling eBooks were self-published independent titles, 10 of Amazon's Top 20 Best Selling eBooks were self-published indie titles., and 56 of Amazon's Top 100 Best Selling eBooks were self-published indie titles, with 20 of the Top 100 priced between $2.99 and $5.99.

When it comes to print books, Amazon reported that the Big 5 hold less than a quarter of the print book bestseller slots, and their unit sales, dollars, and author royalties are less than half of what Amazon's generates through its print business.

Here are seven writers who started out as self-published authors.

1. E.L James is the author of 50 Shades of Grey. The trilogy started out as fan fiction. She posted it on fan fiction sites and her own website. Later, she developed it into an original erotic trilogy. E.L. then self-published the first book as an eBook and print-on-demand paperback through The Writers' Coffee Shop, a virtual publisher based in Australia. From there, the book spread quickly. It took off after the trilogy was dubbed "Mommy Porn" and became a worldwide phenomenon. Of course, we all know the trilogy has been adaptation into screen format, and became a hit across the world, despite heavy criticism for having been poorly written.

2. Science Fiction author Hugh Howey's dystopian sci-fi trilogy originally started out as a short story. He expanded the story and added more installments after publishing the first few through Kindle Direct Publishing. The original series is broken up into nine books. To retain

his e-Book rights, Howey turned down a seven-figure deal in favor of mid-six figure sum.

3. Amanda Hocking is one of the first YA self-published novelists to earn over $2 million publishing only e-books. By 2011, she had sold over a million copies of her nine books and was averaging 9000 book sales per day. In March of 2011, St. Martin's Press offered her a publishing deal worth $2 million, the contract included a four book YA paranormal series called *Watersong*.

4. Lisa Genova is a trained neuroscientist. Genova self-published her book, *Still Alice*, in 2007 with iUniverse; the book was picked up by Simon & Schuster in 2009. *Still Alice* spent over 40 weeks on the New York Times bestseller list and has been translated into 25 different languages. In addition, there is also a film adaptation in the works. Traditional publishers published her next two books, *Left Neglected*, and *Love Anthony*.

5. Stephen King - *People, Places and Things* and *The Star Invaders* were self-published when he was a teenager.

6. Dan Poynter - He wrote more than 130 self-published books, mostly about self-publishing, many selling in the millions.

7. Paul Kingsnorth - *The Wake* - Kingsnorth is an example of how to use new, non-traditional publishing methods as a more flexible alternative for experimental books. He went to crowdfunding, allowing hopeful readers to pledge their support for his work.

The Con's

It is estimated that about 81 % of Americans want to write a book.

A September 2016 report from Bowker, the official ISBN Agency for the United States, and its territories, shows that more than 725 thousand self-published works were registered in 2015. That equals nearly 2000 books a day. There is no doubt, that figure has gone up since then.

You are now the businessperson responsible for marketing, publicity, and presentations. In other words, it is time to put on the businessman's hat. You are about to find out the writing was the easy part.

Keep in mind, even if you find a traditional publisher, most likely, you will still be responsible for all or part of what was previously mentioned. This is especially true if you are published through a mid or small-press publishing company.

THE AUTHORS WEBSITE

Mainstream publishers do not necessarily believe in Author Websites. Often, they think the author is better off creating and maintaining a Facebook page instead. Their take on the subject is that websites are not effective enough for the time put into them.

However, for the self-published author, the story is a little different. Think of yourself as a business. You are your brand. These days, almost any small business should have a website.

WordPress has the most functionality out of all the website builders. Its PHP backend is open to heavy customization. Its user-friendly frontend also allows the user to heavily customize their website using themes and plugins. However, it may take a few days to learn how to get a functioning website going in WordPress. Nonetheless, it is still the best option for the most custom website experience. If you want to have many features like forums, MailChimp integration, SalesForce integration, social media, e-commerce, and multimedia, WordPress is the best option for you.

On the other hand, Website Builders like Wix, Weebly, or those offered by companies like Hostingdude or GoDaddy are the easiest to use. If you chose to build your own website, one of these might be your best bet. You can easily have your website up in minutes. If you do not require a lot of

custom functionality but want to run a simple e-commerce website, multimedia website, or business website, a builder website builder.com is probably the best choice. They are also the best choice if you do not want to spend much time on learning how to manage your website. I personally use Hostingdude (owned by GoDaddy) for my websites and find the functionality of their website builder to be quite easy and self-explanatory.

The Importance of Having a Website

1. Low-Cost Advertising. The World Wide Web has a far greater reach than any other form of advertising. It may take time to build traffic to your website, but it is well worth it, and costs next to nothing to do.

2. Visibility is an important factor of having a website. Once someone hears about you, one of the first things someone might do is research who you are. Remember, you are the brand.

3. Accessibility is important. A website is online and accessible 24 hours a day, 365 days of the year.

4. A website is a great way to generate sales. Your website can sell products at any time. Potential customers are not restricted to business hours. Instead, they can go online and purchase your book whenever they want, or redirect them to a website that sells your work.

5. How the author is researched. As a radio host, I am constantly searching my guest's websites. It gives the author more credibility. Often, the author's website offers autobiographical material, interviews, events, and speeches. It may include book information not found on the purchasing websites.

6. You can create a blog and post it on our website.

7. Contact information. Create a contact page.

8. Where to buy your book. Have links to the various websites that carry your book.

9. Post your book trailer there. Once you have your book published and ready to go, create a book trailer and post it on your website and author webpage wherever your book is listed.

FUNDING YOUR PROJECT

Publishing your work can be somewhat expensive, although it does not have to be. There is the cover that can cost a little. Some individuals will need to pay someone to typeset and/or format their work. Then there are consignment book signings. You will need to have printed books on hand for many consignment shops. In most cases, the biggest expense you will have is for the editing. That will vary based on your writing style and the genre. We will get more into the editing further on in this booklet.

Crowdfunding

Some authors prefer to create a function to promote their work. There is no better way than to have a crowdfunding campaign. Keep in mind, it does take a little effort to make this campaign a success. However, the advantage of presenting a crowdfunding platform is that you get instant exposer for your project, you have the opportunity to pre-sale books, and in addition, you can create an event around your book (a book launching) that may prove too much of an expense otherwise. I always include a book launching as part of the campaign when I set up fundraising sites for fellow authors.

If you choose to create a funding account, you must be willing to invite everyone - family, personal friends, and all your social media friends. When doing so, keep in mind, they will be getting something in return. Some authors feel crowdfunding is like asking for a handout. It is not. In fact, it is the opposite. Depending on how much they donate, they will receive incentives for their participation. The best way to look at it is like this, if they go to the store to buy your book, they may pay up to $20 retail for it. Well, if they donate to your campaign, they will get the same book with your autograph.

Advantages:

1. Each donation is like a pre-sale of your book. That helps to pay for the cover, editor, printing, or other incentives you may be offering.

2. Set up a reception/cocktail hour. You will provide the hors d'oeuvres and non-alcoholic drinks. If they want an alcoholic drink, have a bar available for them to pay. Most people who donate to your campaign will buy more books at the signing/cocktail hour.

3. At the reception, you can invite the media from radio, newspaper, and TV. People you have never met will want to participate so that they can "rub elbows" with an author. "Aspects of

Writing Radio Show" got its start from such an event.

4. Offer "Dinner with the Author" after the cocktail hour. Not all, but some of the people attending the cocktail hour will want to stay over and have dinner with the author. This gives them more of a reason to talk about your books to others.

Kickstarter and Indiegogo are the two biggest platforms for crowdfunding. There are others out there, and I encourage you to explore them all. However, do not get involved with a funding site that asks for money. You should never have to pay to set up an account.

What to look for and do:

1. Kickstarter – Using this funding website, keep in mind, once you set a goal, you will have to make the goal to collect the funds. If you set your goal at $2,000, you must get $2,000 in pledges, or you get nothing.

2. Indiegogo – I like this platform because there are two ways to set up your campaign. With **Fixed Funding**, you keep your money only if you meet your goal. This is the same as with Kickstarter. If you chose **Flexible Funding**, you keep the money pledged to your campaign

no matter what. The difference between the two options is the percentage you will be charged. **Flexible Funding** charges a higher percentage. However, if you chose **Flexible Funding**, <u>and you meet your goal</u>, the campaign will automatically revert to the percentage charged as if you had chosen **Fixed Funding**. I prefer having two options. At least with Flexible Funding you have a chance of raising some money to back your project. "Some" is always better than "None." Please refer to their website.

3. You should offer various incentives that you feel people will want when donating to your campaign. That can range from a signed copy of your book, e-book, thank you on your author website, an invite to a cocktail event, and dinner with the author, and more. See other author campaigns to get a better idea of how to adjust your campaign to fit your needs.

4. Use your email list, social media outlets, business card with a campaign link, and word of mouth to let people know what you are doing.

5. Make a budget before setting a goal. It should include all expenses; event location, food, books, editing, cover design, and any other expenses you can think of. Always factor in

30 % of what you are collecting to cover your expenses, such as printing of books, flyers, posters for the event, etc.

6. Keep in mind you will also need to allow for percentages that the crowdfunding platforms charge. That will usually be about 10% for everything, including collecting the donations by credit card.

7. You want to discourage someone from writing you a check. Do not necessarily turn it down but try and get them to donate on your funding account. The more people donate to your funding platform, the more others will want to contribute. Everyone wants to be on a winning team.

8. Keep in mind, the most of all funding will come in during the last few days of the campaign. That is when you want to hit your campaign/social media outlets the hardest.

9. Never overdo solicitation. In the beginning, once a day is enough. Skip a few days, and then begin campaigning again. Most people will donate on their payday. I recommend that you keep that in mind when you launch your campaign. Also, I would never make it more than a 30-day campaign. If someone is going

to donate, they will do it within that 30-day window.

BECOMING THE AUTHOR
BOOK SIGNINGS

It is important that you dress the part. Do not wear a sloppy shirt or blouse, particularly with stains or holes in them. You do not necessarily have to wear a suit or dress but dress the part. Be well groomed. You are in the public's eye. You are your own star, regardless of how big or small that star is.

Have multiple copies of your book on the table. Make it a nice display. Place your poster beside the table on an easel so that it catches the attention of the customer as they walk through the door.

Greet the customer as they come through the door or approach your table. Some authors prefer to sit, but I would recommend you stand. Do not be afraid to hand them a copy to look at. Do not devote your time talking to someone you already know. If someone sees you in conversation, they most likely will move on. You may not see that person again.

Signing the book:

Most authors sign the title page. Some will sign the inside of the cover, others the cover. Think about how you want to sign your books. Do you want a catch phrase – "Thanks" "Enjoy" Warm Wishes"? You might want to personalize it if you know the person – "To my good friend Max." You may wish to include the date. Whether you use a Sharpie or an ink pen, make sure the ink will dry quickly. You might want to use a blotter sheet (a think sheet of paper) to place in-between the page that you are signing. This will prevent the ink from bleeding through, especially if you choose to use a Sharpie.

Have extra books on hand in addition to what the store may have ordered for you. This is in case you sell what was on hand. Most stores will allow you to bring extra copies in from your car, and they will reimburse you for those books later.

Have someone take pictures. You can use them to post on your social media websites.

If you have room on your table, put out a bowl of candy. That always gets someone's attention.

Another thing you might want to factor into your budget is a complimentary copy of your book for radio interviews and consideration for bookstores, etc.

Follow up your book signings and interviews with a thank you note. You never know if it could lead to referrals somewhere down the road.

CHECK LIST FOR PUBLISHING

Edit Your Book: Find an editor online or ask another author whose book you enjoyed. Look at a book and see if an editor is listed in the credits. Seek out that editor's website.

Library of Congress: A library of Congress Number is not necessary to publish. However, it is easier to get it placed into the library system if you have one. You should apply about two weeks before publication. At that time, you will be assigned an agent. This person will be your contact for all your current and future books. www.loc.gov/publish/pcn

Copyright Registration: You will need proof that the book you finished is truly yours. It takes about two to three months to receive the copyright number after you register, and sometimes longer. You may be able to publish on Kindle without the finalized registration because the case number should be the same as the copyright number. However, it might be safer to wait. A few authors have told me they experienced a problem with listing their work on Amazon without the completed registration. My advice is to register as soon as possible, even if you have to delay your book's publishing date by a few months. Standard Application is $45.00 to $65.00, depending on the work.

www.copyright.gov/registration

ISBN: You want to go to Bowker for your ISBN's. They are the distributor for all ISBN's, regardless of who you buy them. Therefore, why not just go to the source. Once you sign up with Bowker, you will be redirected to Myidentifiers.com. That is their official sight for publishers. And yes, if you self-publish, you are a publisher.

Barcode: You can purchase your barcode from Bowker as well. If you buy them on your www.myidentifiers website, they are permanently attached to the ISBN you used for the barcode.

Cover Design: You can purchase a cover design from several different sources. TheCreativePenn.com offers a host of individual cover designers. Many of the online publisher's offer that service as well. If you can find a local artist or graphic designer, perhaps this might be your best bet. That way you can see the progress as you go. You might want to try websites like https://99designs.com/, https://www.fiverr.com/, or others like them.

Format: We talked about this earlier in the book. Please refer to that section.

Synopsis: The synopsis is especially important. That is how you will get the attention of the reader. The cover, the synopsis and the first chapter (or at least the first paragraph), is how a reader will determine their interest in your book.

Book Pitch: This can be similar to your book synopsis. Just make sure it is something you will remember. It does not have to be verbatim each time, but a clear picture of what your work is about.

Author Website: Post past and upcoming events, list reviews and offer a contact page. Share links where your book is available for purchase.

A Square Account is a must-have for accepting credit card payments at signings and/or for consignment sales. Currently, this is free. Website: https://squareup.com/us/en

Poster: A poster of your book helps. You may even consider having your picture (headshot) somewhere on the poster.

Easel: If you have room on your table, a tabletop easel works fine. For most venues you will need a freestanding easel for your poster.

Post Cards: Have a postcard-sized advertisement for your table. It should feature your book cover, the home page address of your website, and all outlets your book is available online.

Business Cards: Always have a business card available. Hand them out wherever you go, the restaurant, at the grocery store, dental office, bank, everywhere. Do not be shy!

Bookmarks: In addition to handing out a bookmark with each sale, have someone stand outside the store of the event to pass them out. That person should say as they hand out the bookmark, "Would you like a free bookmark?" Once they have it in their hand, tell them, "Just so you know, the author of this book is inside. Go by and meet him/her. He/she loves to chat."

Social Media Accounts: Create a page for your book. Sign up for as many social media outlets as you can handle. Post all your upcoming events. Let your social media friends know when you have a book coming out.

Press Release: Various websites will instruct you on developing an effective press release. Constant Contact and MailChimp offer a great way to distribute your press release via email. Mashable.com offer several places you can place your press release and that offer advertising services. Advisoryhq.com also offers several press release distribution companies.

Book Trailer: If you have the skills, or know someone who does, consider a book trailer. It should not be more than one or two minutes in length. They are a great way to advertise your book. You can place it on your author website, and even the author page of your accounts like Amazon. You can then blast it on your social media accounts and share it with book club websites. More importantly, you can have the trailer playing on a loop at your signing or event.

EIN: This is not necessary to start publishing online. However, if you have an established business, you need to apply for an Employer Identification Number. **https://www.irs.gov/businesses/small-businesses-self-employed/apply-for-an-employer-identification-number-ein-online**.

Sole Proprietor: You can also report tax information for books sold with your year-end taxes using your social security number, especially if you have set yourself up in business as a sole proprietor.

For additional advice: I recommend this link to learn more about what you should or should not do when presenting your book: http://www.writing-world.com. They offer a host of information for self-publishing. However, do not burden yourself with too much information until you have a grasp on how to publish.

IN CONCLUSION

In conclusion, do not be afraid to check out the Internet. There is a plethora of information out there at your fingertips. See what other authors are doing. Check out the latest trend of publishing. Digital publishing is constantly changing. I recommend that you stay clear of the online publishing houses that charge a lot for getting your book to press. They often mark your book at a higher price, making it difficult to distribute and sale to the retail market. Listen to various author interviews to find out what works for them. Find out where other authors have done radio and television interviews. Join a writer's group to learn more about your community of authors. Attend events for writers before you publish to learn what you can do to participate in the future. Ask for reviews from everyone you know. Only use your social media websites for your work - do not get personal. Consider public speaking where you can offer your book for sale or a part of the event. Exchange business cards at every event – network. You might want to consider attending other author signings in your area. Get an idea of what they are doing. But the most important thing to remember is – HAVE FUN AND ENJOY THE RIDE!

ADDITIONAL WEBSITES WORTH YOUR WHILE

https://www.publishersglobal.com/
On this website you will find over 20,000 publishers and publishing services companies in 132 countries to submit your work.

Scrivener
https://www.literatureandlatte.com/scrivener
A software for novelist and screenwriters.

FREE SOFTWARE FOR SCREENWRITERS

Trelby
Causality
Page2Stage
Drama Queen
Dub Script
Studio Binder
Highland Software
Celtx

OTHER SOFTWARE FOR SCREENWRITERS
Fade In
Final Draft
Movie Magic Screenwriter

I recommend Studio Binder to learn more about formatting your script.
https://www.studiobinder.com/blog/brilliant-script-screenplay-format/

www.ingramcontent.com/pod-product-compliance
Lightning Source LLC
Chambersburg PA
CBHW070656050426
42451CB00008B/377